I Can Read

ANNIE RUTH

To Quendell —
love,
Annie Ruth

ruth

CREATIONS

CINCINNATI, OHIO

This book is dedicated to my mama Stella Hampton who passed the legacy of reading to me, my children Cameron & Gerian, and all of the children who dare to dream and learn through reading.
— Annie Ruth

Published by: A. Ruth Creations
for Eye of the Artists Foundation, Inc.
1860 Wynnewood Lane
Cincinnati, OH 45237
(513) 821-9027
www.eyeoftheartists.org
Eye of the Artists Foundation is a charitable, educational and community empowerment organization whose mission is to serve as a catalyst and advocate for exposure to the arts for the entire community, with an emphasis on youths.

ISBN: 0-9656306-7-6

Printed in the United States of America

Our Legacy, Our Gift

Embrace the royalty that flows through our veins! It is the legacy of a great people — the descendants of kings and queens. For thousands of years our people have had a rich legacy of sharing our story – a story told through visual art, literature, song, dance, and a creative spirit.

It is my belief that everyone is creative. By tapping into the creative spirit of our youths, it is my goal to use the art to inspire them to read. As a visual artist and poet I chose to share some of our story through vibrant colors, using simple words to inspire the reader to dig deeper and explore a world called "Imagination".

The I Can Read book and arts education curriculum embraces the spirit of creativity and knowledge. Knowledge is necessary for the survival of any culture and reading is essential for obtaining knowledge.

As you utilize I Can Read to embrace the principle of each one, teach one by encouraging older children to read to younger children, it is my prayer that "with all of your getting, you will get an understanding" (literacy) and share the gift with someone else.

Peace and blessings,

Annie Ruth

Annie Ruth
Founder & President
Eye of the Artists Foundation, Inc.

EDUCATION

I can read at school

I can read at home

I can read with friends

I can read alone

I can read at a library

I can read at the store

I can read outside

I can read on the bus

I can read in a train

I can read at church
I can read in the temple

I can read big words
I can read even simple...

I can read at night

I can read in the day

I can read when I dance

I can read when I play

I can read numbers

I can read a poem

I can read lots of books

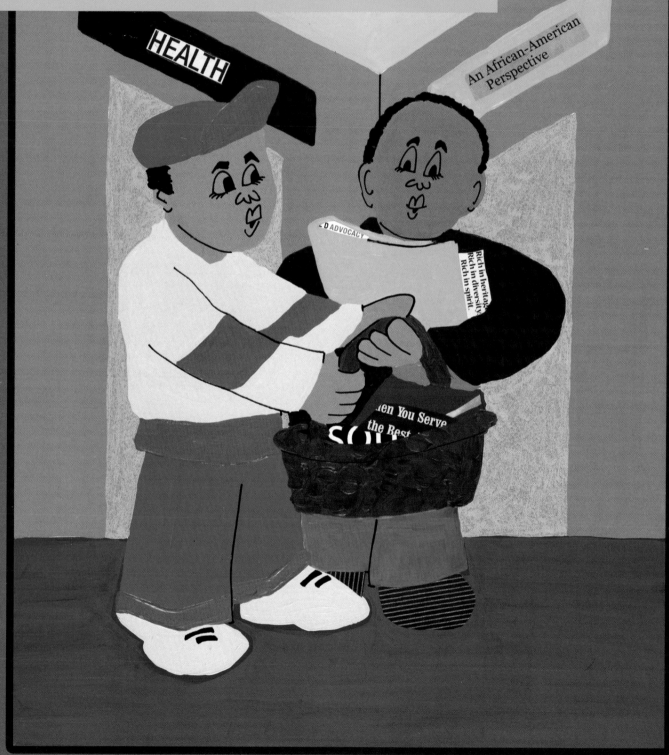

I can read anything...I CAN READ

Literary Art Tip: Playing describes having fun, performing music, taking part in a game, freedom of movement, and so many other things.

EXERCISE: Write a verse, prose, poem, or song describing how you play.
(Example: Describe playing a musical instrument, a song on the stereo, sports, etc.)

SOME ART TERMS

PATTERN - When a shape or form is repeated over and over again.

TEXTURES - The way a surface looks or feels - rough, smooth, silky, etc.

COLLAGE - An artistic composition made by pasting different materials down on a flat surface.

MIXED MEDIA - The use of two or more materials and/or reproduction processes

MEDIUM - The material or technical means of artistic expression. (Oils, watercolors, acrylics, ink, pencil, charcoal, etc.)

SENSES - The (5) five senses are gateways through which the brain gets its entire contact with the outside world. (Hearing, Touching, Seeing, Smelling, and Tasting) The sixth sense is our emotions. Artwork that evokes emotions stimulates the brain

DID YOU KNOW: Gerald Porter founded The Cincinnati Herald in 1955. He died in a car accident and his wife, Marjorie Parham took over. Later, her son, William Spillers, took over operations, and Sesh Communications purchased it from Mrs. Parham's publishing company, Porter Publishing, in August, 1996. In all those years- even when the office was bombed (shortly before SESH Communications bought it), and even after the Sesh office was robbed, the Herald has NEVER missed an issue. It's been a weekly publication since Mr. Porter started it in 1955. Now there are some additional Sesh publications: The Northern Kentucky Herald, The Dayton Defender, and Our Week, which is distributed in 33 cities.

EXERCISE:

"It's not always what you say but how you say it" (This message holds true for **language arts** (the art of words) and **visual arts** (the art of pictures - paintings, photographs, sculptures, etc.) List some things that you can read. Use the pictures, "I can read anything" and "I can read a paper" to help spark your imagination. Write a poem or song using your own words.

HINT: We can use our bodies to communicate. What is that language called? You've got it! It's called body language! Can we read body language?

Cultural Lesson: The Message of the Art

An African **griot,** pronounced (gree - OH) or (gree-OTT) is a man who learns and passes on the story of his people from generation to generation.

His purpose (what he was born to do) is to share the story (the history of his family, clan, or community). A **griot** is like a living history book, who possesses the ability to archive centuries of "oral history", which is almost inconceivable to the western mind. Americans of African descent carry on the tradition of the **griot** through many aspects of our culture, utilizing a technique of "call and response". This unique verbal technique is used in poetry, rap, preaching, and many of our songs and literature.

EXERCISE: In the pictures above, locate the people who are griots. Tell why you think they are griots and how they pass on the history of our people.

DID YOU KNOW: "Njema" in the Kiswahili language of Eastern Africa denotes "good news". Jet magazine, a newsweekly publication, was created in 1951 by John H. Johnson (1918 - 2005) of Chicago's Johnson Publishing Company to "provide blacks with a convenient-sized magazine summarizing the week's biggest black news in a well-organized, easy to read format."

Style

A way of making art that can be described. (A person may have his or her own style, such as in AFRICA; the Egyptians worked in a style that was different from the style of Japanese artists in ASIA.)

Annie Ruth uses a style she describes as direct innocence. She uses this style to create art for and about children, utilizing a bold primary color palette to stimulate their minds and emotions. Within this style she blends collage and mixed media. Some of the items that she uses are acrylic paint, fabric, paper, leaves, shells, sand, and many other things.

Processing your thoughts:

The artwork above is called *"I Can Read"*
Question: What would you name the artwork?

Discussion:
1. Talk about some things that you see in the picture.
2. Why do you think the children are reading things that contain African American history, (like a JET magazine, a newspaper, and a history book)?
3. What are some other words that you can use in place of "read"?

Activity Choice:
1. Create a picture (your own design for I Can Read)
   - Use bright colors and mixed media like paper, paint, colored pencils, markers, fabric, etc. to create your artwork.
2. Write a poem or song for the I Can Read picture.

My Affirmation

I am the descendant of royalty.
I am creative —
I will embrace my creativity.
Because I am created in the image of God, I achieve.
I achieve excellence because of the sacrifices
Of my ancestors who have gone before me and
The paths, which they have paved . . .
And the roads they have traveled.
I will always embrace the knowledge that
I am the descendant of kings and queens.
I have a rich legacy of excellence, education, and intellect —
I honor this great legacy
Through the many books that I read.
This day I affirm that I will keep the torch of knowledge shinning brightly
And I will share this light with others.

Amen.

Let's empower our children with knowledge of who they are

Study African American History

<u>The African Americans,</u> edited by Charles Collins and David Cohen, Viking Studio Books

<u>African American Pride, Celebrating our achievements, contributions, and enduring legacy,</u> Tyehimba Jess, Citadel Press

<u>The African American Odyssey, Vol One: to 1877,</u> Darlene Clark Hine, William C. Hine, Stanley Harrold, 2nd edition

$9.95
ISBN 0-9656306-7-6

9 780965 630672

Descubramos

VENEZUELA